Truth Bomb - Ditching The Lies, Finding The Truth

By Nicole G M

Contents

Introduction

If you're reading this, you're likely tired of the lies that bombard us every day—lies about who we are, our worth, and our potential.

This book is designed to help you identify those lies and, more importantly, replace them with the powerful truths found in God's Word.

A "truth bomb" is an explosive revelation of truth. It's that moment when everything clicks, and you see things clearly.

Throughout this book, we'll explore common lies that the enemy—whether you perceive this as societal pressures, negative self-talk, or spiritual deception—wants you to believe.

We'll dive deep into the Bible to uncover the truth that can set you free.

This book is designed to be practical. You'll find reflective questions, action steps, and scripture references to guide you. Ready to drop some truth bombs? Let's get started.

Chapter 1: The Enemy's Deception

Before we can ditch the lies, we need to understand where they come from. The enemy wants you to believe lies that keep you from living the full life God has for you.

Consider the story of Adam and Eve in Genesis 3. The serpent (representing deception) convinced Eve that God was withholding something good from her. By twisting God's words, the serpent planted doubt and led her to make a choice that brought severe consequences.

Deception often works the same way today. Lies take root in subtle ways, making us question our worth, abilities, and purpose.

But recognizing these lies is the first step to overcoming them. Awareness is key. We must be vigilant and discerning, constantly aligning our thoughts with the truth found in Scripture.

Reflective Questions:

What lies have you believed about yourself in the past?

How have these lies impacted your life and decisions?

Can you identify any specific sources of these lies (e.g., media, peers, internal thoughts)?

Action Steps:

Awareness Practice: Spend a week noting every negative thought or doubt that crosses your mind. At the end of each day, review and categorize these thoughts to see patterns.

Scripture Study: Begin a Bible reading plan focused on understanding God's truth about human identity and purpose.

Prayer: Ask God to reveal any lies you have believed and to help you see the truth clearly.

Chapter 2:

Lie #1 - "I'm Not Good Enough"

One of the most pervasive lies is "I'm not good enough." This lie can stem from comparisons, past failures, or unrealistic expectations.

It can lead to feelings of inadequacy and prevent you from pursuing your God-given potential.

But the truth is, you are enough, you always have been and you always will be.

Truth in God's Word:

"I praise you because I am fearfully and wonderfully made; your works are wonderful, I know that full well." - Psalm 139:14

"For we are God's masterpiece. He has created us anew in Christ Jesus, so we can do the good things he planned for us long ago." - Ephesians 2:10

Practical Steps:

Reflective Question: When do you feel "not good enough"? What specific situations or comparisons trigger these feelings?

Truth Statements: Write down and repeat affirmations like, "I am fearfully and wonderfully made" and "I am God's masterpiece."

Action Steps:

Create a Strengths List: Write down all your strengths, talents, and accomplishments. Reflect on this list daily, especially when feelings of inadequacy arise.

Gratitude Journal: Keep a journal where you note things you are grateful for each day. Focusing on gratitude can shift your mindset from what's lacking to what's abundant in your life.

Seek Feedback: Ask trusted friends, family, or mentors to share what they see as your strengths and positive qualities. Hearing positive feedback from others can reinforce your sense of worth.

Prayer:

"Lord, help me to see myself as You see me—fearfully and wonderfully made. Remind me of my worth and value in Your eyes, and help me to silence the lies that say I am not good enough. Amen."

Chapter 3:

Lie #2 - "I Have to Be Perfect"

Perfectionism is a heavy burden. The lie that you have to be perfect can lead to anxiety, burnout, and a constant sense of failure.

But the truth is, God's grace is sufficient, and you are accepted as you are.

Truth in God's Word:

"But he said to me, 'My grace is sufficient for you, for my power is made perfect in weakness.' Therefore I will boast all the more gladly about my weaknesses, so that Christ's power may rest on me." - 2 Corinthians 12:9

"For all have sinned and fall short of the glory of God." - Romans 3:23

Practical Steps:

Reflective Question: How does the need for perfection affect your life? What specific areas do you feel pressure to be perfect?

Truth Statements: Affirm, "God's grace is enough for me," and "His power is made perfect in my weaknesses."

Action Steps:

Set Realistic Goals: Break larger tasks into smaller, manageable steps and celebrate each completed step, not just the end result.

Embrace Imperfection: Allow yourself to make mistakes. Recognize that failure is a part of growth and learning.

Practice Self-Compassion: Treat yourself with the same kindness and understanding that you would offer a friend who is struggling.

Prayer:

"Lord, thank You for Your grace that covers my imperfections. Help me to let go of the need to be perfect and to rest in Your sufficiency. Teach me to embrace my weaknesses and see Your strength in them. Amen."

Chapter 4:

Lie #3 - "I'm Alone"

The feeling of loneliness can be overwhelming. The lie "I'm alone" can make you feel isolated and forgotten.

But the truth is, God is always with you, and you are never truly alone.

Truth in God's Word:

"Be strong and courageous. Do not be afraid or terrified because of them, for the Lord your

God goes with you; he will never leave you nor forsake you." - Deuteronomy 31:6

"And surely I am with you always, to the very end of the age." - Matthew 28:20

Practical Steps:

Reflective Question: When do you feel most alone? What circumstances or thoughts contribute to these feelings?

Truth Statements: Repeat, "God is with me always," and "I am never alone."

Action Steps:

Reach Out: Contact friends, family, or members of your community. Building connections with others can alleviate feelings of loneliness.

Join a Group: Get involved in a church youth group, sports team, or club where you can meet new people and form meaningful relationships.

Spend Time with God: Cultivate a habit of prayer and Bible study. Use this time to deepen your relationship with God and feel His presence.

Prayer:

"Lord, thank You for Your constant presence in my life. When I feel alone, remind me that You are always with me. Help me to build connections with others and to find comfort in Your unfailing companionship. Amen."

Chapter 5:

Lie #4 - "I Can't Change"

Believing that you can't change keeps you stuck. The lie that you are incapable of change can prevent you from growing and reaching your potential.

But the truth is, with God's help, you can transform and grow.

Truth in God's Word:

"I can do all this through him who gives me strength." - Philippians 4:13
"Therefore, if anyone is in Christ, the new creation has come: The old has gone, the new is here!" - 2 Corinthians 5:17

Practical Steps:

Reflective Question: What areas of your life feel stagnant? What changes do you desire, and what fears hold you back?

Truth Statements: Declare, "I am a new creation in Christ," and "With God's strength, I can change."

Action Steps:

Set Small Goals: Break down your desired changes into smaller, achievable steps. Celebrate each milestone.

Seek Accountability: Find a mentor or friend who can support and encourage you in your journey of transformation.

Embrace Growth: View challenges and setbacks as opportunities for growth rather than failures.

PRAYER:

"Lord, thank You for the strength and new life You offer. Help me to embrace change and transformation, trusting that with Your help, I can grow and become more like Christ. Guide me and give me the courage to pursue the changes I need. Amen."

Chapter 6:

Lie #5 - "My Past Defines Me"

Your past does not define you. The lie that it does can hinder your future and keep you from embracing new opportunities.

But the truth is, in Christ, you are made new.

Truth in God's Word:

"Forget the former things; do not dwell on the past. See, I am doing a new thing!" - Isaiah 43:18-19

"Therefore, there is now no condemnation for those who are in Christ Jesus." - Romans 8:1

<h1 style="text-align:center">PRACTICAL STEPS:</h1>

Reflective Question: How has your past affected your self-view and decisions? What aspects of your past do you need to let go of?

Truth Statements: Affirm, "I am not condemned; I am a new creation in Christ."

<h1 style="text-align:center">ACTION STEPS:</h1>

Write a Forgiveness Letter: Write a letter to yourself or someone else, forgiving past mistakes and letting go of any guilt or resentment.

Focus on the Future: Set goals for your future that align with the new identity and purpose you have in Christ.

Surround Yourself with Positivity:
Engage with positive influences that reinforce your new path and identity.

Prayer:

"Lord, thank You for the new life and identity You offer me in Christ. Help me to let go of my past and not let it define my future. Remind me daily of Your forgiveness and the new path You have set before me. Amen."

Chapter 7:

Lie #6 - "I'm Not Loved"

Feeling unloved is a painful lie. The belief that you are not loved can lead to a deep sense of loneliness and worthlessness.

But the truth is, God's love for you is eternal and unchanging.

Truth in God's Word:

"I have loved you with an everlasting love; I have drawn you with unfailing kindness." - Jeremiah 31:3

"For I am convinced that neither death nor life, neither angels nor demons, neither the present nor the future, nor any powers, neither height nor depth, nor anything else in all creation, will be able to separate us from the love of God that is in Christ Jesus our Lord." - Romans 8:38-39

Practical Steps:

Reflective Question: When do you feel unloved? What experiences or thoughts contribute to this feeling?

Truth Statements: Repeat, "God loves me with an everlasting love," and "Nothing can separate me from God's love."

Action Steps:

Spend Time in God's Presence: Cultivate a habit of prayer and Bible study to deepen your understanding and experience of God's love.

Engage in Acts of Kindness: Show love to others through acts of kindness, which can reinforce your own sense of being loved and valued.

Affirmations: Regularly use affirmations that remind you of God's unwavering love.

"Lord, thank You for Your unfailing love that never changes. Help me to feel and know Your love deeply in my heart. When I feel unloved, remind me of Your everlasting love and kindness towards me. Amen."

Chapter 8: Lie #7 –

"My Value Comes from What I Do"

Your worth isn't based on achievements. The lie that your value comes from what you do can be exhausting and dehumanizing.

The truth is, you are valuable just as you are.

Truth in God's Word:

"For it is by grace you have been saved, through faith—and this is not from yourselves, it is the gift of God—not by works, so that no one can boast." - Ephesians 2:8-9

"This is my Son, whom I love; with him I am well pleased." - Matthew 3:17

Practical Steps:

Reflective Question: How do you measure your worth? What pressures do you feel to achieve or perform?

Truth Statements: Declare, "My value comes from who I am in Christ, not what I do."

Action Steps:

Rest and Reflect: Take intentional time to rest and reflect on your worth apart from your achievements.

Find Joy in Being: Engage in activities that you enjoy purely for the sake of enjoyment, not for achieving or proving something.

Affirm Your Inherent Worth: Regularly remind yourself that your worth comes from being a child of God, not from your accomplishments.

PRAYER:

"Lord, thank You that my value is found in You and not in what I do. Help me to rest in the truth of my inherent worth as Your child. Teach me to enjoy life and find joy in being, not just in doing. Amen."

Chapter 9:

Lie #8 - "I Have to Conform to Fit In"

Conforming to fit in is a common lie. The truth is, that you are uniquely made and don't need to conform to be accepted.

God created you with a unique purpose and identity.

Truth in God's Word:

"Do not conform to the pattern of this world, but be transformed by the renewing of your mind. Then you will be able to test and approve what God's will is—his good, pleasing and perfect will." - Romans 12:2

"But you are a chosen people, a royal priesthood, a holy nation, God's special possession, that you may declare the praises of him who called you out of darkness into his wonderful light." - 1 Peter 2:9

Practical Steps:

Reflective Question: When do you feel the pressure to conform? What makes you unique, and how can you embrace it?

Truth Statements: Repeat, "I am chosen and special in God's eyes," and "I do not need to conform to be accepted."

Action Steps:

Celebrate Your Uniqueness: List the qualities that make you unique and thank God for each one..

Renew Your Mind: Regularly meditate on scriptures that affirm your unique identity and purpose in Christ.

Prayer:

"Lord, thank You for creating me uniquely and for a special purpose. Help me to resist the pressure to conform and to embrace the identity and purpose You have given me. Guide me to people and places that support and celebrate who I am in You. Amen."

Chapter 10:

Lie #9 - "I'll Never Be Happy"

The belief that you'll never be happy can lead to a sense of hopelessness and despair. This lie can keep you from experiencing joy and contentment.

But the truth is, true happiness and joy are found in a relationship with God.

Truth in God's Word:

"You make known to me the path of life; you will fill me with joy in your presence, with eternal pleasures at your right hand." - Psalm 16:11

"The joy of the Lord is your strength." - Nehemiah 8:10

Practical Steps:

Reflective Question: What are your sources of happiness? How do they align with God's promises and truths?

Truth Statements: Repeat, "God fills me with joy," and "The joy of the Lord is my strength."

Action Steps:

Cultivate Gratitude: Keep a gratitude journal, writing down things you are thankful for each day. Focusing on blessings can increase your sense of joy.

Pursue God's Presence: Spend time in worship, prayer, and Bible study to draw closer to God and experience His joy.

Engage in Joyful Activities: Participate in activities that bring you joy and align with your values, such as hobbies, sports, or spending time with loved ones.

PRAYER:

"Lord, thank You for the joy and happiness that come from knowing You. Help me to find true joy in Your presence and to focus on Your blessings. Teach me to cultivate

gratitude and to seek happiness in ways that
honor You. Amen."

Chapter 11:

Lie #10 - "I Have No Purpose"

Believing you have no purpose can lead to feelings of aimlessness and despair. The lie that your life lacks meaning can make it difficult to find motivation and direction.

But the truth is, God has a unique plan and purpose for each of us.

Truth in God's Word:

"For I know the plans I have for you," declares the Lord, "plans to prosper you and not to harm you, plans to give you hope and a future." - Jeremiah 29:11

"For we are God's handiwork, created in Christ Jesus to do good works, which God prepared in advance for us to do." - Ephesians 2:10

Practical Steps:

Reflective Question: What are your passions and talents? How can you use them to serve others and glorify God?

Truth Statements: Affirm, "God has a plan and purpose for my life," and "I am created for good works."

Discover Your Gifts: Take time to explore and identify your spiritual gifts and talents. Consider taking a spiritual gifts assessment.

Set Meaningful Goals: Write down specific, achievable goals that align with your passions and God's purpose for you.

Serve Others: Find ways to volunteer and serve in your community, church, or school. Serving others can help you discover your purpose and bring fulfillment.

Prayer:

"Lord, thank You for the unique plan and purpose You have for my life. Help me to discover and embrace my gifts and use them

to serve You and others. Guide me as I seek to
fulfill the purpose You have set for me.
Amen."

Chapter 12: Tools for Ongoing Victory

Living in truth is an ongoing journey. Here are tools to help you stay grounded in the truth and ditch the lies:

Daily Practices:

Scripture Reading: Start each day with a Bible verse that speaks truth. Use devotionals or Bible reading plans to guide you.

Prayer and Meditation: Spend time in prayer, focusing on God's promises and seeking His guidance.

Affirmations: Use truth statements daily to reinforce your identity in Christ. Write them down and place them where you can see them regularly.

Building a Support System:

Mentors and Friends: Surround yourself with people who speak truth into your life. Seek out mentors who can guide you and friends who encourage you in your faith.

Community Groups: Join groups where you can share and grow together. Church youth groups, Bible study groups, or other faith-based communities can provide support and accountability.

Daily Practices Recap:

Start each day with a Bible verse and prayer.

Use affirmations to reinforce your identity in Christ.

Engage with supportive communities and seek guidance from mentors.

Conclusion

As we reach the conclusion of this journey together, remember that the truth is your most powerful ally.

The lies you've confronted are not just challenges; they are stepping stones toward a life of freedom, joy, and purpose.

By recognizing and rejecting these falsehoods, and by embracing the truths found in God's Word, you are forging a new path—a path where you are no longer bound by the deceit of the enemy, but empowered by the unwavering truth of who you are in Christ.

Living in truth is a daily commitment. Each day brings new challenges and potential deceptions, but you are now equipped with the tools and wisdom to stand firm.

Let the scriptures, affirmations, and practical steps you've learned be your guide. Surround yourself with a supportive community, seek God's presence continually, and remind yourself of your inherent worth and purpose.

Your journey toward truth is ongoing, and each step you take brings you closer to the life God has uniquely designed for you.

As you move forward, embrace your God-given identity and purpose with confidence and courage. You are loved, valued, and capable of incredible things.

The truth of God's Word is your foundation, enabling you to overcome any lie the enemy might throw your way. Let your life be a testament to the transformative power of truth.

Keep seeking, keep growing, and always remember that you are fearfully and wonderfully made with a unique purpose on the earth. There has never been anyone like you and there never will be anyone like you. So choose today to trust in God's plan, and live boldly in the freedom and victory that His truth provides.